A MESSAGE FROM MARY

PS NAVADA

PSNAVADA

A Message from Mary

Copyright © 2018 by PS Navada

Published by PSNAVADA

Title ID # 8312477

ISBN – 13: 978-1987485196

ISBN – 10: 198748519X

Cover photo of Loch Ness taken by author

❀ Created with Vellum

Thank you to those Mary chose
to assist with this book:
Simone and Tammy

FOREWORD

I was raised a Lutheran, but I always had an affinity for Mother Mary, I never have nor will refer to her as "Mother". I felt her presence with me long before we began communicating. I felt her loving and supporting others through me, especially those dealing with issues of fear, anger and self-esteem. She always felt quite sisterly in fact, and we both shared our eternal love of Jesus, who was always present as well. His was the first voice in Spirit that I heard as clearly as if he were speaking next to me and I felt his arms around me.

More than one intuitive told me I would be writing a book with Mary someday and I certainly had that in the back of my mind. The day she wanted to begin writing was unmistakable and well planned. I write my own material as well, and I can say with certainty that her voice and mine are not the same.

I am ever grateful to have her by my side in my work and our work together. I am honored to have her share her incredible wisdom, love and support through me any time she wishes.

A MESSAGE FROM MARY

Here begins the written transmission of my LOVE and SUPPORT to the human embodiments of our Light. I am merely here to remind you of who you are, that you may readily and effortlessly access it.

My goal is to be seen as your Sister in Light, your Sister in Spirit. Always supporting, never judging. I will be with you until you recognize and know that I am You, and You are Me, until you no longer need a reminder or crutch.

It is not lost on me that a great number of you have always cast me in the role of intercessory. I was never between You and God but a bridge to your GodSelf. I am honored to be that symbol of Grace, Unconditional Love and Faith. Allow me to step down from the iconic pedestal and embrace you in your own Light and Glory.

The concept of us all being brothers and sisters in

light is integral to living a life of Spiritual Grace and Abundance. Whether parents, children, spouses, lovers and friends, we are all first and foremost brothers and sisters. All other relationship dynamics are simply vibrational playing fields. The adage "All the world's a stage" is an apt representation.

We come to this realm with our roles formatted by ourselves in the ethers. We match our goals and "schoolings," for lack of a better word, with our brother and sister families. Such joyful reunions as we meet between incarnations. If I could impart to you even a fraction of that Joy and understanding, all your tensions and concerns would fall away.

The time continuum that creates the reality of this earthly home is like a tidal ebbing and flowing which the oceans depict for you. There are crescendos in time where great understanding and vibrational advancements occur. They are also very disruptive and cataclysmic at times. Only your own vibrational understanding will determine your experience. Less expanded souls will feel more confined and defined at these times by their circumstances.

The era of the Christ awareness, which you most recognize me from, was one of these times. We are in the midst of another now as we seek to abandon all belief in separateness from the Light and from each other.

Those with expanded consciousness are the pioneers.

Fortunately, that expanded consciousness also gives you the tools to transition with detachment from the physical egoic state of earth. It is that detachment which brings Grace and Ease, not just for yourselves but for all others. Your acceptance soothes the distress that other confined souls are experiencing.

Remember your physical form and human-ness is a culmination of memory and anticipation from all you have experienced before. All the former realities of those harsher times, those times of denser vibration are carried with you until you consciously, by choice, release them. As your vibration expands you must shed them as an unnecessary skin. We cannot peel them away for you. Bless them, create ceremony to honor them if necessary, and release them.

To replace an adage "What would Jesus do?" ask "What would my Unlimited Spirit do?" What would you desire and accomplish if you dropped all those confines and limitations. Create from a place of Love and Joy and, yes, Sensual Pleasure. To create a loving, gracious and beautiful existence on this earthly plane would be your graduation, your crowning glory. Make peace with your appreciation of the pleasures of the physical world. Why else would you be here? Earth is the reflection of our physical desires as Spiritual beings.

I wish to impart to you the love and acceptance I have for you. I want you to receive it as from one friend to another, one light being to another. We are

One. Receive my honoring of you for this journey you've chosen. Allow yourself to see yourself from my vantage point. That is the only difference between us, our vantage point.

I am floating in the space of pure Love and completeness. You are in a space you perceive as separate. When you can bring that Love and completeness to your being, your human being, you will flourish. You will have heaven on earth.

We feel as if we are nearing the finish line with many of you. So many of you are so close to releasing the limitations and receiving the magnitude of yourselves. This last leap is huge.

Remember, there is nothing to fix about any of you. All you need is to release all the judgment and have full acceptance of the human conditions you have worked your Spirit Self through. See it as an obstacle course. Each lifetime you have had a certain skill set to achieve your goals. In each lifetime, you have hobbled yourself in defined ways to steer you through choices you might have avoided. Understand that YOU have been the conductor of this journey. You are the conductor and the orchestra. The director and the actor. It is you on the stage.

When you understand you are ready... You are ready. Ready to call in all the infinite light, all the infinite skills you have learned in each lifetime and even in the observations you have made from our vantage place between lifetimes.

Now, to release all the human trappings that are based on this false reality, release the belief that your past experiences and human truths confine you to old outcomes. Understand you will also release old desires that had their foundations in fear.

Let go of all you have been. And see what your infinite Light Self desires in Joy. How your Infinite Light Self chooses to perceive this playground Earth. Step into this place of Light, Love and Completeness and Create from here.

Can you let go of all the judgments, consequences and punishments you have created to lift your experience to where you are now? If you can receive this message and understand its truth, you are ready. You are ready to pioneer the New Reality of Light and Love on earth.

We want you to cultivate and master the male-female, yin-yang of your existence. Again, having no judgment and having acceptance and detachment will allow you to master the path of Joy to reality.

As you rest in Joy and desire the creation of your perfect life, it is flowing from you as a river. This river, like flow of Joy, is creating the pathway. It is a very feminine fluid state of being.

Now call in your clarity and your intuition—a marriage of male and female to do the negotiations into physical reality. Together, your clarity and intuition will create the proper circumstances for manifestation.

The third step is that then your authority and logic, male side, chooses the actual footholds and maneuvers to capitalize on these circumstances. Logic will organize your journey, your day, your order of events and timeline.

Now, you rest back into Joy, creating the next "moment" from that same place.

You cannot imagine how excited we are to be co-creating with you. When you expand to hold your Greatness, your infinity, there is no separation from us. We are again brothers and sisters flowing as one. You have access to not only all that you are but also to all that we are together.

And Yes! You are the lucky ones, the bless-ed ones. You are in the physical realm, in physical form, experiencing all the delights of Eden. If we were capable of envy, we would envy your physical experience. But, Oh, how we honor you and the journey you have made to arrive here! I hope you feel our Gratitude for being a part of it.

Breathe in deeply, allowing the blessed air to reach all the way to your belly. Gently hold the breath in your expanded lungs. Feel the blessings of that breath course through your entire being. As you finally exhale, release that blessing with gratitude to the world around you and Mother Earth beneath you.

You are a fountain. Always full, always receiving,

always releasing. Always blessed. Always being blessed. Always blessing. You are the blessing--with every breath, every footstep, loving and blessing Mother Earth, our beautiful host.

She adorns our altar every day with blooms and blossoms, leaving droplets of water like dew. She shares her kingdom of beings and wealth of minerals. She daily rolls out vast carpets and vistas and pathways.

Treat our beautiful hostess as the altar she is, to our Eden, our vision of Paradise. Co-create with her the oasis of beauty on every corner and walkway.

A powerful tool in manifesting a perfect divinely aligned life is to understand that this present moment is the creator of YOUR NEXT MOMENT. Rest peacefully in the present moment. Know that you did the best you could to create these circumstances, this reality. Be in acceptance and gratitude.

Breathe in Peace and our Love and support. Claim divine alignment with Joyful Purpose. You are now in the cycle to create magic. Acceptance Gratitude Peace and Joy.

Here I am in Light and completeness, ready to assist you. Step into this place and feel your own completeness. You need nothing. You are whole and are simply requiring the Universe to reflect your complete Joy and Divinity mindlessly, nonspecifically, while in this space.

This is not the arena for details. This is where you

embrace and become Bliss and Joy. Anchor it in and around you. I am here as if a guided meditation. Allow me to assist you into this magical space. Dwell here as long as possible, as often as possible. It is expanding your vibration.

The real, authentic you is perfect. We cannot move forward until you accept this completely. Sit with that mantra until you feel no resistance to it.

Note that you are not claiming to be delighted with all your choices and interactions to this point, but you accept them as the stepping-stones of your human journey. Until all of your cellular being is qualified in the Light of acceptance and judgment-free Love, you will be bound by earthly laws, the laws of ego and gravity.

Surrender every judgment as it is sensed with Love and acceptance. Each moment of this acceptance creates more of your completeness in Love and Joy.

Put on blinders and just keep greeting and releasing every negative thought and limitation into Love and Light. Simplistic, repetitious and Powerful.

In every moment, remember to use us. Delegate the responsibilities of oversight to us. We will gently remind you of your new CHOSEN pathways. We will help you release the old habits that do not serve the new you.

Many of your habits, and even desires, are based on old fears. Many of your desires are merely the coping mechanisms of the feeling of incompleteness.

Affirm your Love, Light and Completeness with every breath and then ask for our assistance in maintaining that vibration as you walk through your day. We will happily point out how the old habits are not relevant. We wish you many happy AHA moments.

You will experience more grace and ease as you walk more firmly in Joy and Light each day. Remember each moment that you rest in Faith, Love and Joy is creating the path and future experiences. Don't be dismayed by the challenging moments. They will become fewer and fewer with Joy fueling your new way of being.

Please remember to not judge your progress in ascension. We will use that term henceforth to mean Heaven on Earth.

The word Moment is so important here. Being joyful in every moment possible is creating your next moments. We acknowledge you do experience difficult moments. Let the discomfort, dissatisfaction or anger pass through you and return to Grace by handing your concerns into the hands of Faith. Then you can come back to creating joyful outcomes.

Be aware of judging your progress in the moment. That is what can give the perception of a roller coaster, as if gripping the rails too tightly and being thrown about. Just bring your habits to the forefront and keep putting one joy filled step with joyful anticipation in front of the other. The state of grace is a field around you and can only be seen from the peace of detachment.

Honor your desires and wants; then they will never become needs.

Every moment you spend in Peace will anchor you more securely in that field of grace and conscious manifestation.

In troubling moments, be swift in expressing the negative reaction, anger, fear or doubt and then move it to the place of concern. Concern is a very short step from Faith. Release your concerns to Faith. Now, breathe in Peace again, knowing you are creating your next moments from that State of Grace.

Peace is the Playground for Joy.

Have you ever invited your own Spirit to fill you before?

As you distract your mind in a chosen meditation form, allow the joy of your own Spirit to fill you. Did you know your own Joyful Spirit is God Source? Ask and receive. This is YOU. Do you feel broken or "less than" now? Of course not!

Your own God Self lies all around you, waiting for you to feel worthy and asking to connect. It is your birthright, your God right. Can you accept your sacredness, your divinity and your joy?

Physical activity is perfect for tiring out your human-ness. Exercise, move, work and dance! Release the static energy! Use it up. Joyful friction and static! Come to the place of rest. Don't judge your physical being and energy. Accept, amuse and distract it. That energy and momentum is crucial to your joyful existence here. Make friends with it. Get on the same page of joyful creation and expression.

Call on me to help you! My energy has a special quality to it, the "flavor" of my being, if you will. It is of course, unconditional Love. My energy and love is available to you now, in this moment. Allow it to douse with Love, the smoldering coal of a distrust, shame, sadness or grief. I love you unconditionally, right now, as you are, in anger, in sadness or shame. Receive my Love and heal that you may stand radiant in your own divinity.

To be free you must lose judgment. Meet judgment face on, in every moment, with Love. If this is your assignment, your homework should keep you very busy for quite a while!

In every second of the day, your heart is always the conduit for our expansive Love. It is only through your hearts that ANYTHING can pass through from this side. By bridging your own feelings and attaining detachment you can be the fountain of so much Love and Healing. In Love, great vibrational healing can occur. Only through detachment can you see and participate consciously.

Being in the moment is a powerful and purposeful thing if done consciously. It often includes honoring the present circumstances seemingly affecting you. To be in the moment is to acknowledge your perception that the circumstances "happened" to you. Changing your understanding to know that YOUR past "moments" brought the present as it is now. Understand this and bring back your Peace in the moment to create your future.

Be still, be peaceful in the moment. This is desirable compared to moving forward mindlessly. Moving forward mindlessly leaves you vulnerable to all random flotsam and jetsam flowing in your path. It is better to be still and peaceful until you have clarity-- something to move towards knowingly, consciously.

When in doubt, do something joyful that will fulfill you in your darker moment or time of limbo. Reach for what knowingly gives you happiness. Elevate your vibration, so your clarity can find you sooner.

May I help you redefine Faith? Faith is you filled with you. With your Divine presence and knowing. When you are filled up with Light, with all the dark corners washed away, you are left with no questions-- only the momentum of your Joy and desires. Like a child, no fears, no doubts and no second-guessing.

Move steadfastly towards Peace and Joy. With only that motive, and your "in the moment' monitoring, you are guaranteed success.

Treat yourself lovingly. Treasure your physical being and desires. It is your vehicle in this human paradise. Allow it to relish and enjoy. Know in every moment…. You can create Bliss.

I truly want you to simplify your quest. Understand

that you consciously tune in with your breath, in the moment, and become aware of what you are giving your attention to. Love it, honor it, celebrate it and be grateful for it. Heal it if necessary. Ask for clarity if it is an obstacle. Send it Love. Breathe in Peace. Exhale gratitude.

You have so many cheering you on from this side. so many waiting to be asked to be of assistance. You will find special bonds and affinities with many of us. You have been here in our shoes before as well and will remember us all as a team, a family. When you accept our homage to you, you will receive so much more. As an equal!

Each expansion of your vibration puts you into a new consciousness and perspective. It will initially be unfamiliar, as when you get a new prescription for eyeglasses. Give yourself time to adjust. Do not retreat. Just be still and observe your world through your new perspective. You will be aware of new solutions to old obstacles, and you will see that some obstacles have simply disappeared. Do not hunt for them. Move forward with gratitude. You may find new objects lie in your path. Delight in observing them and discerning their meaning. You are ever fuller of Grace.

Always regard your body, your human home, as the vessel of God's Grace and a Joy. In every moment release judgment and fill yourself with Peace. Then you are a vessel and conduit of Love and Joy. This is not a selfless act. It is Your Joy and perfect life that wishes to express and appear for you. Do this for your own Divine expression, that you may create Your Heaven on Earth. Focus on the moments, so the hours and days will unfold from Grace.

Judgment is the opposite of your "I Am" Divine self. Each soul has created the circumstances and relevant companions to go through their own qualifying process. You do not need to participate in or judge any one else's journey. You will find yourself in enough arenas of interaction for your own.

Truth is merely fearlessness.

Patience is not about time. It is about being patient with your human-ness to accept your divinity.

At times, it is helpful to do General house clearings of your four bodies--the physical, emotional, mental and spiritual. Close your eyes and allow yourself to be swept away, out of the way, so all the corners will be accessible.

Ask your Divine Self with the assistance of the Angels to sweep away everything that does not serve your new path and intentions of Joy. This is an opportunity to release obstacles without observation, thereby avoiding judgment.

Every space you clear may now be filled with Light, Peace and Love. You are ready to foster more Joy!

I promise that by following these new ways of being in the moment, you will begin to have moments of inexplicable Joy. Treasure these. Bask in them. They are the anchoring pins of your new self. Stop and bask as if you just felt the sun's rays for the first time on a cloudy day.

Can you imagine a life where you move purposefully and joyfully in the direction of your dreams, joys and pleasure? A life in which you understand that you create everything you see and know. A life where you understand the lessons and obstacles you have placed in your path. A life of empowerment and joy as you clear your way to Peace and Divine alignment.

Patience is more than waiting. It is moving towards what is worth your attention.

Patience is such an interesting term. It denotes suffering or sacrifice. Could we make it another outmoded four-letter word? Replace it with acceptance of the now, and the resulting un-foldment of joy, as we gently request that ego drop the reins of our beautiful chariot carrying us through our human existence, and lovingly hand them to our Joy. Patience becomes the story of our journey.

You are writing the story of your human life in every moment. Each breath in is a new page. Fresh-- with a feeling of joyful anticipation! Breathe in Peace. Exhale gratitude. You are still in the game. Let go of doubts and fears. Embrace Joyful anticipation. Transform. Watch and transform.

You are not becoming aware of your limitless, eternal and joyful Spirit to escape your present circumstances. As you feel your Real presence, you bask in it. Invite it to create from the moment, every moment forward. It is from that place of limitless possibilities that this world and its circumstances are formed.

Become your own bridge between your perfect joyful essence and your human expression. Be the loving, all-knowing conductor of your human experience as the orchestra. Be the loving, all-knowing director of your human expression as a play on a joyful stage--all roles and parts for your adventure.

Being one with God, with your Divine Light is Heaven. Expressing that through all your thoughts, desires and every cell of your being is Heaven, Heaven on earth. Ascension. It becomes not about going home. It becomes about bringing home here.

ABOUT THE AUTHOR

Pamela Sonda Navada is an intuitive who has worked with clients and groups for years. She communes with Angels and Ascended Masters. Pamela now does group work, speaking engagements, writes and travels.

She may be contacted through her website at psnavada.com or pamelasondanavada.com

54272443R00017

Made in the USA
Columbia, SC
28 March 2019